This book is primarily designed for children aged 8 to 14 but is also suitable for older readers including adults. Easy to understand, it adds a new and refreshing dimension to the history of Reigate and Redhill over the past 300 years.

REIGATE AND REDHILL IN BYGONE DAYS

By Tony Powell

Above: *Crown steps in Reigate at the dawn of the Twentieth Century. Note the costumes worn by the girls.*

Front cover: *Reigate Market Place in the early nineteenth century seen from the White Hart Inn in Bell Street.*
The Swan Inn is on the left of the picture.

REDHILL CENTRE
FOR
&Local Family History

ISBN 0 9537532 1 2

Printed by
Rayment Printers Limited, 5 Horsham Road, Dorking, Surrey RH4 2JN

**Published by: Redhill Centre for Local & Family History
Redhill Library, Warwick Quadrant
Redhill, Surrey, RH1 1NN
Tel.no. 01737 773204 Fax no. 01737 778020
e-mail:redhill.info@dial.pipex.com
http://www.surreyweb.org.uk/redhill-history-centre**

Somers Hall in Slipshoe Street, Reigate, beside the old Red Cross Inn. Victorians named the street believing that Medieval pilgrims descending from the North Downs into Reigate eased off their sandals. However modern historians have questioned the existence of a "Pilgrims Way" along the Downs, although it remains a popular local tradition.

"The key to a nation's future is in it's past. A nation that loses it has no future. For men's deepest desires – the instrument by which a continuing society moulds it's destiny – spring from their own inherited experience. We cannot recreate the past but we cannot escape it. It is in our blood and bone. To understand the temperament of a people, a statesman has first to know it's history".

Arthur Bryant

OTHER BOOKS

By the same author

Fire over England
Published 1988

Other books in the series

The History of Redhill Technical School   Tom Slaughter
1926-1966
Published January 2000

Royalists, Roundheads and Rogues   Brenda Potter
Their connections with Reigate in the 17th Century
To be published June/July 2000

Redhill, Reigate and District Family History
Guide to Local Records   Arthur Hawkes
To be published September/October 2000

Tudor Times in Reigate   Tony Powell
To be published November/December 2000

CONTENTS

ABOUT THE AUTHOR

Tony Powell was born at Redhill General hospital in 1942 and has since lived in Reigate all his life. From 1953 he was educated at Reigate Grammar School. Between 1953 and 1959 he was very involved in the Reigate Pageants and grew up very interested in history.

Between 1956 and 1971 he was a leading light in the South Park Young Stagers (S.P.Y.S) and founded Reigate Youth Theatre in 1977. During the 70's he was a founder committee member of the local arts council. More recently he has served as Chairman of the Showtime at the Harlequin Theatre up to his resignation earlier this year to allow more time to concentrate on these history books.

About three years ago Tony and his solicitor friend Chris Bell felt the need for a series of local history books and had the idea of applying for a lottery grant to cover the cost of publication. Shortly after it was decided to ask Jackie Johnson, Chairman of the Redhill Centre for Local and Family History to take charge of the project. News that a grant had been approved was received early last year.

AUTHORS INTRODUCTION

At the start of last year I was asked to write a history of Victorian Reigate & Redhill with Peter Carr, a local teacher as my advisor. Sadly Peter had to drop out but before he did so we had agreed to extend the period back to 1700 to include the Georgian period, the Regency, and the Napoleonic era when so many changes took place in the district to create Reigate and Redhill we know today.

The most important event, locally, in Victorian times was the coming of the railways which in turn led to the development of Redhill. To really understand the reasons for this all important choice of route it is necessary to go back to the Georgian and coaching era and the rise of Brighton.

Peter Carr expressed the view that this book should be used by schools for the literacy hour. I am inclined to agree with the view that the literacy hour should always be used to kill two birds with one stone and teach children history at the same time as teaching them to read.

I want to thank Peter Carr for all his help with the early chapters of this book. Also for the team who have worked with me on this project. Firstly there is Jan Hines who typed the text and inserted the corrections and Chris Le Quesne who accepted responsibility for the editing and desktop publishing. This was no easy task with so many illustrations. Also Arthur Hawkes who spent many hours scanning all the illustrations, Chris Bell for proof reading and Jackie Johnson for organising the project overall. It's been a tough job but it was worth it to see our efforts in print.

I feel that thanks and credit are due to the Holmesdale Natural History Museum for providing the illustrations on pages 16 and 47. Also the Surrey History Service for permission to reproduce the illustrations on page 48, and Robert Norrington for permission to use the illustrations on pages 9, 11, 12, 17, 18, 28, and 71.

Finally I would like to thank the Heritage Lottery Fund for making this project possible.

Tony Powell
(May 2000)

CHAPTER 1

AN INTRODUCTION TO EARLY REIGATE

The towns of Reigate and Redhill, our towns, nestle in the Vale of Holmesdale between the North Downs or hills to the north and a smaller range of hills to the south. Reigate is a very old town but Redhill has only existed for about 150 years, since it grew up as a result of the coming of the railways in 1841.

A long time ago, long before the Romans came to Britain, there was a road or trackway along the top of the North Downs from east to west and later people travelled along the vale of Holmesdale.

Travellers in these early days would either walk, ride on horseback, or sit in a cart drawn by a horse. Sometimes the very rich would travel in a litter drawn by a horse or carried by people who were called slaves.

Travel to the south of Reigate was not possible in these early days because of a great forest called the Weald, or wild place. The trees, mostly oaks were very dense and the ground was covered in brambles and thorn bushes. For many years people did not go into the Weald as it was the home of wild animals including wolves. The name Woodhatch means the gate to the Weald.

We do not know when the first settlement was built at Reigate; but it was before the Norman Conquest in 1066 and at that time Reigate was called Cherchefelle. It was part of the land belonging to Queen Edith who was the wife of King Edward the Confessor. The name Cherchefelle is in the famous Domesday Book compiled for King William the Conqueror in 1086. One hundred years later the name was changed to Reigate.

In these early times there was no hot and cold running water so that people lived beside rivers and streams. The other nearby settlements were at Buckland, Gatton and Merstham and all of them were built beside streams fed out of springs flowing from the base of the North Downs.

Cherchefelle was built beside the Wray stream; parts of which can still be seen today. From the North Downs the stream flows to Wray Common and you can find part of the stream between the Fire Station and the Colman Redland Centre. Other parts of it can be found between Church Walk and behind the east side of Bell Street. The stream flows underground from Bell Street to the Priory Lake. In 1621 the Lake was described as "a fair pond well stocked with fish and a small brede of herons". The stream flows out of the Priory Lake to become the Wallace Brook, or Wally, which meanders through meadows and is crossed by country lanes before joining the River Mole at Flanchford Mill. At one time the stream flowed across Bell Street and people who walked across the ford were used to getting their feet wet.

After the death of Queen Edith her land passed to King William and when he died his son, William Rufus, gave Cherchefelle to a very brave Lord called William of Warenne who was later made Earl of Surrey. The Warennes kept Reigate and were Earls of Surrey for over 250 years.

By 1140 the Warennes had constructed Reigate Castle. It was one of four castles built in Surrey to guard the road to Canterbury where the Christian church was based. The other castles were at Farnham, Guildford and Bletchingley.

About one hundred years later they also built Reigate Priory as a place for monks to live and work. The work of the priory included tending the sick, teaching and a welcome rest place for weary travellers. So it remained for 300 years, long after the last of the Warennes had died.

In the 1530's the Priory was closed down by King Henry VIII and it was rebuilt as a home for the Lords of the Manor. The most famous people to live there were the Howards of Effingham, father and son, William and Charles, who were Lord High Admirals of England to Queen Elizabeth I. Charles Howard commanded the English fleet that defeated the Spanish Armada. Both are buried in the family vault at St Mary's Parish Church in Chart Lane.

By this time Reigate Castle had fallen into decay and local people were taking away the stones to build their own houses and garden walls. This had been happening for a very long time and by 1770 very few of the walls and towers remained.

In 1770 a wealthy man called Barnes built the castle gateway in the castle grounds out of stones from the original castle. Today, the gateway is all that is left of the castle but, if you go into the Castle grounds, you can still walk in the old moat or climb onto the old mound. The grounds are

Reigate Priory today – The Priory museum is open on Wednesdays and Saturdays on the occasions of special exhibitions. The eagle courtyard is behind the left of the picture.

preserved as a garden for peaceful leisure as are those of Reigate Priory.

The old Priory was altered again in about 1700 and that is the building you can see today. By this time it had become a stately home for wealthy local residents. A special feature of the re-building was the twin eagles, taken from the coat of arms of the Parsons family who lived in the Priory about 1700 which can be seen on the gates of the school playground.

All this time Reigate had been a very quiet, secluded place, tucked away between the hills. Apart from wealthy people and soldiers the locals seldom travelled out of the district. A town and market had grown up between the Castle and the Priory, and fairs were held on a regular basis.

The twin eagles can be seen in the rear entrance courtyard at Reigate Priory. The eagles are from the coat of arms of the family who owned Reigate Priory 1681 – 1741

Many of the local people depended on the oatmeal trade for a living. Several small windmills were built around the town to grind oatmeal and larger windmills were to be found on the outskirts at such places as Trumpet Hill, Cockshot Hill and Blackborough Road. Two of these windmills, on Reigate Heath and Wray Common, still exist. The windmill on Reigate Heath is used today as a church.

Reigate Parish Church of St Mary is as old as Reigate itself. At the start of the 1700's a local vicar named Andrew Cranston founded England's first public library in the church. The library, with many ancient books, still exists.

The name Cranston is preserved in Cranston Close on the Woodlands Estate at the top of Cockshot Hill. Lymden Gardens, on the same estate, recalls John Lymden who was the last Prior of Reigate Priory.

Many of the roads in Reigate and Redhill recall the local history of the district. Near Reigate Station are Holmesdale Road and Warren Road. To the south of the town are Howard Road and Effingham Road, named after the Lord High Admirals of England, also St Mary's Road was named after the church. The castle gives it's name to Castlefield Road by the Town Hall and Castle Drive in Woodhatch. Priory Road was one of the earliest roads to be built in South Park. Can you find these roads on the local map?

If you go out for a walk in Reigate, visit the Castle grounds and look for the stone eagles at Reigate Priory. Can you find the parts of the Wray stream that are still visible and where the stream runs in and out of the Priory Lake? When you see the stream remember that it was the reason why Reigate was built where it is.

Have you been over to Reigate Heath and seen the old Windmill Church? If you walk through Reigate Town and see the Holmesdale Building Society in Church Street you now know that it was named because Reigate was built in the Vale of Holmesdale. Go into the Building Society and look at the aerial photos of Reigate.

St Mary's Parish church, Reigate

was built in the Vale of Holmesdale. Go into the Building Society and look at the aerial photos of Reigate.

Reigate Heath at the turn of the present century. The windmill is now used as a church. The hill on which it stands was once known as Galley Hill where it is believed a gallows once stood.

CHAPTER 2

EARLY GEORGIAN REIGATE
(TOWARDS THE REGENCY)

The Regency is the period of history between 1810 and 1820 when King George III went mad and his son, Prince of Wales, was made Prince Regent of England. It was a very important time for Reigate because of the new Brighton Road which led to the events that created the town of Redhill.

To understand this we need to go back to the year 1700 and look at Reigate in the eighteenth century, or as it is sometimes known the "tricorn" period, because of the three cornered hats that people wore. Reigate's Old Town Hall, so well-known in the middle of the town, was first built a few years before 1730, as a market house. An earlier market house had stood at the west end of the High Street between West Street and Upper West Street known at that time as Middle Row and Pudding Lane.

The decision to move the market and market house to the middle of the present town was made at a time when the local oatmeal trade was at its height. Most of the oatmeal was transported out of the town and sold to the London markets or the Royal Navy to make biscuits for the sailors.

A local prison existed at that time on the site of the Samaritans building which can be found half way up the Crown Steps behind 'Our Price Records' shop. Later it was moved to the market place beside the old Town Hall and in 1811 it was re-built as the Cage Prison in Cage Yard beside Safeway. The building still exists, can you find it?

Before the late 1600's the roads were in a bad condition, very muddy in wet weather, and the subject of many complaints by travellers. In fact, very few people travelled and nobody wanted to pay for proper roads. In the towns the streets were built of bumpy cobble stones and street lamps were lit by candles.

By this time a new method of transport had evolved. This was the coach and horse. Very rich people owned their own coaches and employed their own coachmen, but most people who travelled by coach had to pay, just as we have to pay to use a bus or train today.

The White Hart Inn, Reigate, with Bell Street in the background. 1775

The Angel and Tollgate at Woodhatch. Note the wagon in the background

Travelling usually took several days and coaches would stop overnight at coaching inns in the towns and villages. There were several coaching inns in Reigate including the Swan (High Street) and the White Hart (Bell Street). The White Horse, in the middle of Dorking is still the same as it was in the days of horse drawn coaches.

Another method of transport, used in the towns and very big houses was the sedan chair which was carried by two servants.

Goods and farm produce were still carried from place to place in wagons and hay wagons, or wains and these were a common sight in the countryside.

Just before 1700 a new system was devised to pay for the upkeep of the roads. This was the Turnpike or Toll system which meant that roads were paid for by people who used them. Gates were placed across the roads at various places with toll houses where money was collected from the people who wanted to use the road. Early toll gates in Reigate were on Reigate Hill near the Yew Tree pub, and at Woodhatch beside the Angel. The road through Reigate was turnpiked as far south as Crawley in 1697

Buckland village to the west of Reigate on the Dorking Road.

The old tithe barn and pond at Buckland

but beyond there lay only the heart of the impassable Weald which, at that time, was still in many parts, a forest.

At this time the roads were very lawless and travellers lived in fear from highwaymen and footpads. Some of the earliest highwaymen were Royalist Cavaliers whose intention was to discredit and discomfort Cromwell's Roundheads. Highwaymen waited on lonely roads for coaches and held them up with loaded pistols to rob the wealthy passengers of money and jewellery. We believe the terms "Stand And Deliver" and "Your Money Or Your Life" were used. Perhaps the best contemporary description of highwaymen is in John Gay's 'The Beggars Opera', first performed in London in 1728.

"Let us take the Road,
hear the sound of coaches,
The hour of attack
approaches,
Advance my boys and load..."

HIGHWAYMAN'S
CHORUS -
BEGGARS OPERA

The gate to Reigate Park where it is
believed Roly Poly lay in wait for his victim

Reigate Heath is believed to have been the favourite local haunt for highwaymen and footpads. Footpads were a poorer version of highwaymen who loitered in dark places on foot rather than on horseback and used cudgels rather than pistols. They also had fewer scruples regarding who they robbed, rather like present day muggers, whereas highwaymen only robbed rich people.

The hill on Reigate Heath where the golf club and Windmill Church now stands was known as Galley Hill, perhaps because it is believed a gallows or gibbet once stood there or nearby for criminals to hang in chains as examples to others that they should not commit crimes.

About 1729 a local highwayman nicknamed Roly Poly was hanged for murder of a Crawley farmer named Coecock. Roly Poly robbed and killed the man and fled to Epsom where he was caught with his victim's watch and money in his possession. The incident proves that even in those days, before we had a proper police force, crime did not pay.

Another local highwayman seems to have been no less a person than the Landlord of the White Lion public house, a Mr Filewood. The White Lion in Linkfield Street is reputed to be the oldest pub in the district. The Landlord tried to rob a traveller from Brighton, having put wire between the horseshoe and the hoof to make the horse go lame, and substituted the gunpowder in his pistols with bran. The traveller discovered the ruse, reloaded his pistol and shot the landlord dead as he

Sedan chair

tried to rob him at the spot where Ringley Park Avenue meets Reigate Road, then known as Ringley Oak.

Highway Robbery died out following the coming of the railways between the 1820's and 1840's to be replaced on occasion by railway robbery!

Another famous lawless activity at that time was smuggling. This was the distribution of cheap tax free goods brought by ship from France and carried inland by pony. Smuggled goods usually included wines, spirits, tea, tobacco and luxury goods such as lace. Smuggled goods for Reigate were usually stored at Crawley or Copthorne. Items for distribution in London were hidden in a cave at the top of Colley Hill just north of Buckland. The cave has since been filled in.

Coaches in the early 1700's

Smuggling was not seen as a crime by most people who did not like paying taxes and many locals were very sympathetic to the "Gentlemen of the Night" as they were called.

"Five and twenty ponies
Trotting through the dark -
Brandy for the Parson
Baccy for the clerk;
Laces for a lady, letters for a spy
And watch the wall my darling while the Gentlemen go by"

RUDYARD KIPLING

The quietest route from the villages of the Weald to the smuggler's hideaway on Colley Hill would have been through the village of Buckland and it was about this time that the legend of the Buckland Shag became well known locally. The legend told how a strange and fearsome beast known as a 'Shag' or 'Water Horse' lurked in the depths of a lonely pool beside the stream known today as Shagbrook. Several stories were told of encounters with this frightening creature and it is very likely that the stories were put about by smugglers and their local sympathisers to scare people away from the area on dark nights when smuggling runs were being made.

Stage Wagon. 1700's

A lamplighter in the days of candlelight

The scanty forces of law and order responsible for impeding the smugglers were known as "preventative men" who included the Revenue men from Customs and Excise led by a team of "riding officers". In the early 1700's they were easily threatened or bribed by the smugglers who were always more numerous. Later they were induced to be more honest by offers of generous rewards and help from the Army and Royal Navy.

About 1780 a Mr Walter, who was Chief Revenue Officer at Horsham, together with his assistants, Mr Hubbard and Mr Jenden, decided on a plan to foil the local smugglers. He recruited about twenty dragoons and several paid spies. Using inside information he located and took possession of smuggled goods bound for concealment in the very heart of the Weald at St Leonard's Forest near Horsham and Ashdown Forest near East Grinstead.

Soldiers uniforms in the mid 1700's

In the Summer of 1781 he made a successful seizure at Reigate as well as other places including Crawley, Worth and Ditchling, sometimes capturing as much as 2 ½ tons of tea in a month.

After the start of the Napoleonic Wars the Army and Royal Navy were drawn more and more into preventative activities against smuggling and several battles took place. Smuggling finally died out in the 1840's when the Prime Minister, Sir Robert Peel, abolished most of the taxes on smuggled goods with the result that "the Trade" was no longer profitable.

In the 18th century, medical progress remained in its infancy. Less than 100 years earlier the superstitious public had considerable faith in the most incredible cures for illness. Some cures involved crushed spiders and frogs as medicines. By the early 1700's the most popular cure for illness or seeking better health was known as "taking the waters" at the established spa towns that were springing up all over the country. Earlier, in the late 1600's during the restoration, the most popular local spa town was Epsom, renowned for the famous Epsom Salts found in the spring water or wells. Most of the young Cavaliers from London had moved into the area and it

Costume of the gentry in the mid 1700's

Dr Richard Russell at Lewes

soon became a fashionable pleasure town. This fashionable habit later moved to Bath in Somerset and Tunbridge Wells in Kent where bathing in the spa waters or drinking it became central to the social life of the wealthy people of the time.

In 1750, Richard Russell a doctor from Lewes, visited Brighton and decided that sea water was the cure for many ills. He advised the use of the water for both bathing and drinking. Within the next few years most of the London aristocracy and nobility were flocking to Brighton to sample the famous cures.

Of course, the big problem was that to travel from London to Brighton it was necessary to go via Caterham, Godstone, East Grinstead and Lewes as this was the only road and because the toll road south of Reigate led only as far as Crawley. The increased traffic to Brighton was the reason

Fashionable Spa Town in the Eighteenth Century. Tunbridge Wells

it was decided in 1755 to cut a path through the forests of the Weald and extend the road from Crawley to Brighton. It was a decision that would lift Reigate out of its earlier isolation. With the opening of the new road across the Weald the story of Reigate's local history was to change beyond recognition.

On the Brighton Road, the "Old Times". Note the post horn

Napoleon Bonapart – Emperor of France. He set out to conquer much of the world and by 1809 was master of almost all of Europe. He was over ambitious in his attempts to invade Spain, Portugal and Russia. Britain stood alone against him for many years. He was finally defeated by the Duke of Wellington at The Battle of Waterloo in 1815, forced to abdicate and exiled to the island of St Helena where he later died. During the Napoleonic Wars England, especially the South East, was under constant threat of invasion. The presence of French privateers and warships in the channel meant that communication by sea was dangerous, so many new roads and canals etc. were planned during this period.

CHAPTER 3

THE NAPOLEONIC AND REGENCY YEARS

The French Revolution which began in 1789 with the storming of the Bastille in Paris and the long years of warfare, known as the Napoleonic Wars, between Britain and France from 1793 to 1815 were to prove crucial to the history of Reigate and the founding in the 1840's of the new town of Redhill.

The Prince Regent – afterwards George 1V

In the early years of the war Britain was dependent on the Royal Navy for defence of our island shores and to carry the war to the

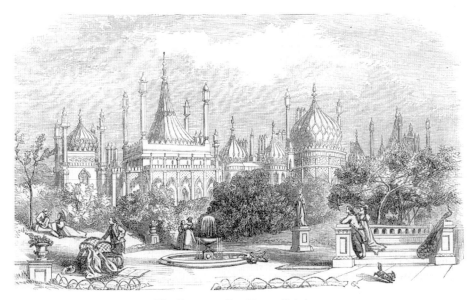

The Regency Pavilion – Brighton

R.E. Norrington

Trees on Earlswood Common remind us of the time when south of Reigate was dense forest before the trees were cut down to clear the land and build ships.

enemy in all parts of the world. A powerful navy had existed since the defeat of the Spanish Armada by Admiral Howard of Effingham, a Reigate man, in Tudor times. The fleet of great ships was called the wooden walls of England more commonly known as Hearts of Oak.

It took as many as 1,000 oak trees to build a first rate battleship, or man of war, and many of these trees were taken from the once great forest of The Weald. Over the years the trees were cut down to make way for farming, provide wood for charcoal burning, to feed the furnaces of the iron works of the Weald and, finally to build the great ships of the English Navy.

The clearance of the Weald had been taking place since Anglo Saxon times, before the Norman Conquest of 1066, but after the Tudor times of the 1500's this process escalated. By the time of the Napoleonic Wars only a few small forests such as Ashdown, St Leonards, Tilgate and Worth remained to the south of the Surrey and Sussex border. Dense forest had given way to the lush green farmlands that we know today despite difficulties in cultivating the heavy clay soil.

Many of the place names to the south of Reigate recall the existence of the great forest. As well as Woodhatch there are Hartswood, Earlswood, Outwood, Charlwood and Norwood Hill. The names of the roads on Wates Estate at Dovers Green; Ashdown, Arden, Delamere and Sherwood are named after forests and on the Meadvale Estate, Hornbeam, Blackthorne, Holly, Willow, Arbutus, Oak, Larch and Juniper, after trees.

The clearance of the Weald made it possible to build more roads from north to south. The road between Crawley and Brighton was the main example since it provided a direct route between London and Brighton at a time when the resort had become fashionable for visits by the London aristocracy and gentry.

The Prince of Wales, later to become Prince Regent and subsequently King George IV, first visited Brighton in 1783 as a sea cure. It was to be the first of many visits that were to add to the success and prosperity of the resort. He built the famous Regency Pavilion as a seaside home and pleasure palace.

Admiral Lord Nelson who defeated the French at the Nile and Trafalgar.

Perhaps we can imagine him and his courtiers travelling through Reigate and maybe stopping at local inns. His favourite inn at Reigate was the White Hart in Bell Street. It is possible that he may have stopped at the Angel at Woodhatch beside the old toll gate.

The Battle of the Nile (1798) The English ships were built from oak.

The Switchback Road, Earlswood Common

The Angel public house dates back to 1600 when it was first built as a bowling alley. It later became an inn called the White Horse. The name was changed to the Angel because of the special coins designed with angels on them which were used by travellers to pay their tolls.

As the war continued, French privateers made it both difficult and dangerous to transport goods through the English Channel to London, and it was decided to dig a canal connecting Portsmouth with the river Wandle at Croydon which flows into the Thames at Wandsworth. Had this been done the canal would have flowed through the Reigate area. The plans were scrapped on account of expense and the danger of damaging the many industries dependent on the Wandle at that time. However, it is of some local interest that John Rennie, father of Sir John Rennie (See chapter 6) was involved in planning the enterprise.

"The Comet" was the most famous stagecoach to run between London and Brighton

Instead the canal was to be replaced with a primitive form of railway from London to Portsmouth on which the wagons were drawn by horses. The first stretch of line, the Surrey Iron Railway, was built from Wandsworth to Croydon and opened in July 1803. It was the world's first public railway since any company could transport their goods in their own wagons for the payment of a toll.

Two years later the rails were extended from Croydon to Merstham under a second company known as the Croydon, Merstham and Godstone Railway. At some points it was necessary to dig cuttings through the North Downs where one of the workmen was killed in a landslip. Goods carried on the railway included coal, limestone, chalk, clay, sand, bricks, stone, flints, Fullers Earth and dung! The conveyance of stone known as Malmstone or Firestone from the Merstham Quarries to London for important building sites goes back to the middle ages. The buildings included St Paul's Cathedral, Windsor Castle and London Bridge.

Admiral Nelson's victory over the combined fleets of France and Spain at Trafalgar in 1805 destroyed the risk of invasion. Therefore the proposed extensions of the iron railway to Godstone and through Reigate to Portsmouth were never constructed; however the old iron railway to Merstham remained in use up until 1838 when it was sold to the London and Brighton Railway Company.

Meantime the steep gradient of Reigate Hill, and having to drive through the narrow cobbled roads of Reigate town, especially having to go around the former site of Reigate Castle was proving a frustration to the ever increasing numbers of travellers making the journey between London and Brighton. In 1809 a toll road was built from Merstham to Reigate via Gatton Point, the present Croydon Road and Gatton Park Road. In 1816 a new toll road, the

The White Horse Coaching Inn, Dorking, showing the arch through which coaches are led into the yard.

*Cutting and Suspension bridge,
Reigate Hill*

present A23, was proposed to run from Croydon alongside the iron railway through Merstham and the future site of Redhill to the Chequers at Horley.

The road over Earlswood Common between St John's (then known as Little London) and the present Causeway Public House (previously the Nags Head) was known as the "Switchback road" on account of its humps or small hills.

Soon after the new road was opened the Lord of the Manor, Lord Somers, allotted a small piece of land at the corner of Mill Street (then Water Lane) and Pendleton Road (then called Union Road) for his nephew, James Cocks, to build a new coaching inn called the Somers Arms.

Coaching Inns were an important part of everyday life to the travelling gentry in Georgian times. A coach would be driven through an arch into the inn yard where men or boys, known as ostlers, would unharness the horses and lead them to the stables for watering, feeding, and a wash and brush down. The passengers would alight and take refreshment of beer or ale and perhaps a roast meal. This would be a welcome relief after sitting for hours in a cramped coach. Overnight accommodation would also have been available.

At the Somers Arms it was usual for passengers to climb the footpath to the top of Redhill Common and enjoy the magnificent views across the valley towards Redstone Hill or south across the wide plain of the Weald while their horses were being cleaned and refreshed before they continued their journey to or from the coast. On fast journeys the horses were simply changed.

The life and usefulness of the Somers Arms was short lived as the coaching trade died down following the opening of the London to Brighton Railway in 1841. For some years after its closure the building was used as a vicarage for the newly built St Johns Church.

In the following years a sharp rivalry built up as the two roads competed for tolls and several changes were made to the original road including the cutting away of the top of Reigate Hill where the suspension bridge now stands. The most significant change to the road was Reigate Tunnel, cut through the Castle Grounds in 1823 to enable traffic to go straight through the town. At the time it was said to be a considerable feat of engineering.

The Napoleonic Wars took a cruel toll amongst the younger generations of the local gentry. William Jolliffe purchased a manor and lands at Merstham in 1788. Ten years later his youngest son, Lt George Jolliffe RN. was killed serving in HMS Bellerophon under Lord Nelson at the Battle of the Nile in 1798. George's cousin, Captain Charles Jolliffe was killed at Waterloo in 1815 having served in several campaigns including the Peninsular War where he was badly wounded at the Battle of Orthes, Southern France, in 1814.

Jolliffe's eldest son, Hylton Jolliffe, was a captain in the Coldstream Guards. He was more fortunate and survived the wars having served in Ireland, Holland and with Sir Ralph Abercromby in Egypt when Napoleon's army was defeated at Alexandria in 1801 and expelled from Egypt.

Perhaps the most notable local casualty was Major Charles Edward Cocks, The eldest son of Lord Somers, who was killed serving under Wellington in the trenches at the siege of Bargos, Northern Spain, in 1812. Cocks had served as an Intelligence Officer throughout the Peninsular War. He was MP for Reigate and had he survived he would have been the next

Tunnel Road, Reigate

lord of the manor. After Cocks had been killed, the Duke of Wellington said he believed that had he outlived the Campaigns, which was virtually impossible due to his exposure to the French artillery, he would have become one of the first Generals in England.

The extent of local casualties amongst the ordinary people of Reigate may never be known. During the wars more common soldiers died of disease than in battle. In 1809 the British had decided to invade mainland Europe by landing troops on the Dutch island of Walcheren in the mouth of the Scheldt. The campaign proved a failure when thousands of British soldiers were stricken with what became known as Walcheren fever. The survivors were brought back to England where a large number were brought to the manor of Linkfield in Redhill which was used as a hospital.

The Napoleonic Wars ended when the Duke of Wellington defeated the French under Napoleon Bonaparte at Waterloo in 1815. After this event Britain and Europe remained at peace for almost 100 years.

British Soldiers of the Napoleonic and early Victorian years

The Prince of Wales became Prince Regent in 1810 when his father, George III was stricken with madness. He became King George IV in 1820 and died in 1830. The Royal Pavilion at Brighton is the best monument to his memory. His regular trips to Brighton had established Reigate as a staging post from North to South as well as East to West. However, the iron railway and new road directly south of Merstham were to prove important to the future development of the area.

A typical middle class Victorian family at home

CHAPTER 4

THE EARLY VICTORIANS

George IV died in 1830 and was succeeded by the ageing William IV who was famous as the Sailor King. During William's reign most of the debates took place in Parliament to decide the location of the main railway lines. William died in 1837 and was succeeded by the young Queen Victoria who would remain on the throne for 67 years and who died in 1900.

King William 1V

What was it like to live in Reigate during the reign of William IV and at the time of Queen Victoria was crowned? Much can be learned from the popular novels of Charles Dickens such as Oliver Twist, A Christmas Carol, Nicholas Nickleby, David Copperfield and The Pickwick Papers.

Reigate Town, known as the Old Borough, consisted of the High Street, Bell Street and a cluster of shops and houses around West Street and Upper West Street formerly known as Middle Row and Pudding Lane, also Park Lane formerly called Workhouse Lane where the old workhouse had once stood on the site of the houses now known as Makepeace A and B. (See colour photographs)

A workhouse was a place where vagrants and the poor were sent to work for their keep. Life in a workhouse was hard and living conditions extremely bad. Food was of very poor quality. This, it was said, was deliberate policy to discourage people from wanting to be kept. The start of Charles Dickens 'Oliver Twist' describes life in a workhouse.

That poverty had been on the increase since the late 1700's was mainly due to the Enclosures Act of the 1770's and subsequent Industrial Revolution. In 1794 the workhouse, together with another at Shaws

Oliver Twist in the workhouse asking for "MORE" - from the novel by Charles Dickens.

Corner, was moved from what is now Park Lane to a new and much larger site on Earlswood Common. Work included the manufacture of blankets and coarse woollens including rugs and wagon tilts, or sending out men to dig the foundations of local roads. Responsibility for running the workhouse was with the parish. When several parishes combined to run a workhouse it was known as a union. Later this would become the site of Redhill General Hospital and more recently a housing estate in the St John's area next to the Earlswood Arms. It was known at the time as the Reigate Union and, as well as Reigate, included the parishes of Nutfield, Headley and Horley.

Poverty in England worsened after the end of the Napoleonic Wars following the discharge of thousands of soldiers and sailors, many of whom were disabled. As the Industrial Revolution spread towards mechanised farming unemployment and homelessness increased. In the early 1830's there were serious riots in nearby Dorking and throughout Sussex and West Surrey. The spread of poverty was accompanied by a massive increase in the population.

In 1801 the population of the Old Borough was approximately 923 people living in just 206 houses. That is an average of five people per house. Most of the houses were located above and between shops and the only large houses were the Barons in Church Street and Browns Lodge in West Street. Of course, the children in those days did not leave home before they married and couples often lived with and looked after their ageing parents so that there were twice as many occupants in a house as you will find today.

Some of the old shops in Reigate still exist and in Bell Street the Ancient House Bookshop, the Bell Public House or Maureen's Fashion shop will provide a good idea of how they looked.

Shops at that time were usually small private, local businesses where the owner would usually live on the premises. There were no chain stores or 'big names' such as you find today and most of them were retailers who sold goods over the counter. Often the goods were cooked or made on the premises.

Go to the Library and find a copy of Palgrave's Illustrated Handbook to Reigate and look at the advertisers in the back pages to see who was advertising in 1860. John Millers' Tea Establishment in the High Street imported tea direct from China. Golden Boot in the Market Place offered the largest and most varied stock of boots and shoes in the neighbourhood and R Bonny, Pastry Cook and Confectioner was established in 1808. W E Green in Bell Street was the watch and clock maker. He was also a jeweller and silversmith. Skilton and Charlwood in West Street offered "genuine home made bread from the best flour".

The outskirts of Reigate Parish were known as the Foreign Borough and included all of Reigate to the north of the Castle Grounds as far as the present Bridge House Hotel and suspension bridge, the manors of Colley and Santon from Colley Hill down to Flanchford Bridge, Reigate

The early Victorian poor

Ladies costumes of the period

Priory and Park together with Woodhatch as far south as Sidlow Bridge (but excluding Hartswood Manor, which was part of Buckland) Meadvale (then known as Mead Hole), Earlswood including the common and Redhill Common and the rural manors of Linkfield, Hooley, Frenches and Redstone on the former site of Redhill. In 1801 the population of the Foreign Borough was 1,323 living in 228 houses.

Reigate was very much a country town and a market town, so people lived close to the cycle of nature that made a community surrounded by farms and rural life.

Since lighting consisted of only a few candles in the early hours of the dark evenings the people usually went to bed very early and rose early in the morning to start work in their shops or on the farms. Virtually all the food that people ate was grown or reared locally including cattle, pigs, sheep, poultry, fruit, vegetables and corn to bake into bread. Milk, butter and cheese were provided by local dairy farms. Cows were milked and the milk delivered or turned to butter and cheese by young girls known as milk maids.

There were no Chinese or Indian foods, or Italian pasta or pizza or hamburgers in Victorian Reigate. Food at that time consisted mainly of roast beef, mutton, pork, and poultry for the more wealthy and chops, sausages and broth for the less well off. Bread, cheese and pies were part of the staple diet. Tripe (from the belly of a cow) and onions was a popular dish as was rabbit stew.

The more wealthy people of the time typically fed on pheasants, lobsters and ducklings. Their desserts often consisted of jelly, blancmange, and a dish of cream and liqueur whipped up to make a delicacy known as syllabubs.

All ages would drink beer and since lager did not exist in those times most meals were washed down with ale. Fizzy and concentrated drinks had not been invented but still, undiluted mineral drinks known as cordials had existed since Tudor times and were extremely popular.

We must remember that in the early 1800's there was no television, radio or cinema, nor were there any supermarkets or electricity, so life was very different to the way we live today. Without home entertainment, and there are no records of any local theatres, people were dependent on local customs and festivals to brighten up their lives and these were more numerous and more enthusiastically supported than today.

The shopfronts of Maureen and The Bell in Reigate remain much the same as they were two hundred years ago.

Then, as now, Christmas was the most important festival and a time of considerable festivity in which feasting on poultry played an important part. It should be mentioned that at any time of year poultry was a luxury available only to the reasonably wealthy. It was also a very religious occasion and a time of charity when everybody was encouraged by the church to think of those less well off than themselves. At that time the only Church of England church in Reigate was St Mary's Parish Church.

For most people, the Christmas holiday lasted twelve days with a special highlight at midnight on New Year's Eve. This is when the church was lit by candles and the bells pealed out and most people gathered around to see in the new year. Twelfth Night was an important occasion because it was the last day of the holiday and, like Christmas, was reserved for special feasting.

St Valentine's day was, until the mid 1800's, less special than it is today. Shrove Tuesday, the last day before the start of Lent was very important. Sadly, details of those old customs have not been well recorded for Reigate but we have vivid details for nearby Dorking. It was usually a day of rough games in the town centre, often involving much cruelty to live poultry. However, in Dorking and other towns in Surrey, it was the occasion for a very rough game of football with the entire male population joining in before the pancake bell was sounded and the women raced each other through the cobblestone streets tossing pancakes from frying pans in anticipation of a good feast for all.

Easter was a deeply religious occasion and May Day was a very popular holiday and perhaps the most English of all festivals. It was seen as the start of summer and meant that people had survived what were, in the olden times, the most dangerous months of the year. Most people who died of illness in these times did so in the cold and wet months of winter.

May Day was a time of spring flowers, of May Queens and Maypole dancing, and morris dancers when people dressed up as Robin Hood or St George and there was also 'Jack of the Green', a figure draped in foliage, to liven up the festivities.

The 29th of May was Oak Apple Day. This was a celebration of Charles II hiding

F. BUDGEN,

WHOLESALE, RETAIL AND

FAMILY GROCER,

TEA-DEALER,

ITALIAN WAREHOUSEMAN,

MARKET PLACE,

REIGATE.

THE CROWN, COMMERCIAL INN, MARKET PLACE REIGATE.

W. BONNY

Respectfully invites the attention of the Inhabitants and Visitors to Reigate, assuring them they will find every comfort and accommodation, at the above House.

Cheerful Private Sitting Rooms and first-rate Beds and every comfort combined with moderate charges.

CHOICE WINES AND SPIRITS,
BOTTLED AND DRAUGHT ALES.

JOSEPH CHANDLER,

Butcher,

BELL STREET, REIGATE.

OPPOSITE THE WHITE HART HOTEL.

A page of advertisements from Palgraves Illustrated Handbook to Reigate 1860

in an Oak tree to escape the Roundheads after the battle of Worcester. The actual date recalls his restoration to the throne in 1660. It was the custom to place a bough of oak on the church tower and for men and boys to wear sprigs of Oak and apples in their hats and caps and shout "Shikshak" at anybody who failed to don these trimmings.

In an age when few people travelled and holidays were practically unheard of, the longest day, 21st and Midsummers day on the 24th of June were important occasions for celebrations. September was the time for harvest festival and another occasion for worship followed by the church harvest supper.

Most significant was November 5th, still celebrated as Guy Fawkes day and preceeded by St Crispins Day on 25th October, which is the anniversary of the Battle of Agincourt, and All Hallows Day on 31st October. In themselves these were occasions of much rowdiness and were a time for shopkeepers to board up their shops and stand by with damp blankets and buckets of water since the roughest elements of locals rolled lighted barrels of pitch through the town and lit their bonfires in the market place amidst scenes that were nothing less than riots.

The Milkmaid's dance on May Day

This was in the days before the district had its own police force and local officials were appointed by the Parish. The Parish official responsible for law and order was known as the beadle who is best described as Mr Bumble in Charles Dickins' 'Oliver Twist'. The first recorded beadle for Reigate was John Keasley in 1727. In October 1807 Thomas Jenkins was appointed beadle "for the purpose of suppressing the many daring insults and offences committed against persons and property of the said Borough". At this time when local officials were appointed by the Parish, each district decided which positions needed to be filled and this varied from place to place. In Dorking there was a Beggar Poker and an Ale Taster!

Cartoon of a parish beadle

A popular local custom toward which the local authorities showed approval and, indeed participated was beating the bounds. At a time when few people had maps and even fewer were sufficiently educated to read and understand them it was important for all men and boys to know the parish boundary by heart. Every so often the men of the district marched out, accompanied by the parish officials, often including the vicar, and the younger boys of the district, to follow the parish boundary giving the youngsters occasional slaps and knocks to jog their memories. This was a vastly enjoyable occasion since the procession marched to the beat of drums and with flags and banners flying.

In 1809 the Parish was presented by the Lord of the Manor, Lord Somers, with its first fire-fighting appliances. These would have been the primitive hand pumping horse drawn fire engines, and six men were employed to work them.

In 1838 the town had its first gas lighting when a local company was formed with its office and gas works in Nutley Lane. Twenty eight public lamps were lit in the town between dusk and 5 am. The town would need

Queen Victoria at the time of her coronation in 1837

to wait another twenty one years for a proper supply of fresh water. In the meantime water continued to be drawn from wells and streams or delivered by a water cart.

On 4th October 1837 the young Queen Victoria visited Reigate in the course of a journey by coach from Windsor Castle to Brighton. The town was decked with triumphal arches and flowers and the people gathered in the town waving flags and cheering in fervent declarations of loyalty to the new monarch. It was in the same year that Parliament had agreed to build a railway through the future site of Redhill.

Triumphal Arch in Bell Street for Queen Victoria's visit 1837

Redhill looking towards the common. A rural setting before the coming of the railways

Old cottages in Linkfield Lane, Redhill, close to the site of the old Manor House.

Makepeace A & B in Park Lane were Lady Henry Somerset's dower house, built on the site of Reigate's earliest workhouse.

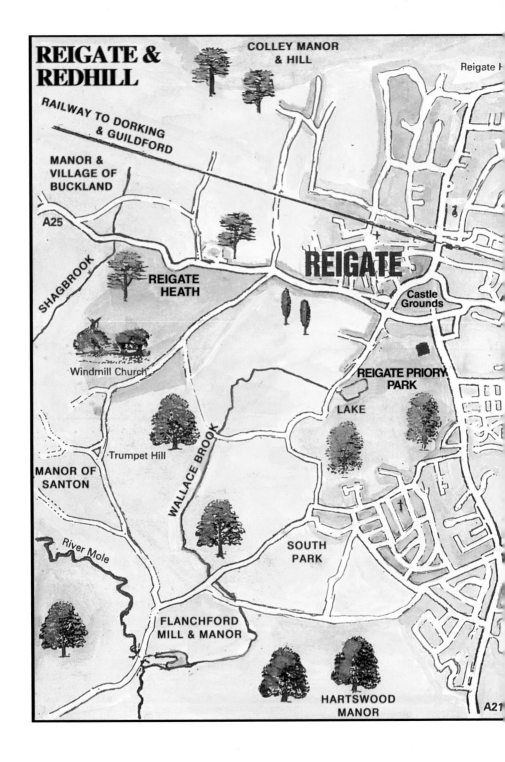

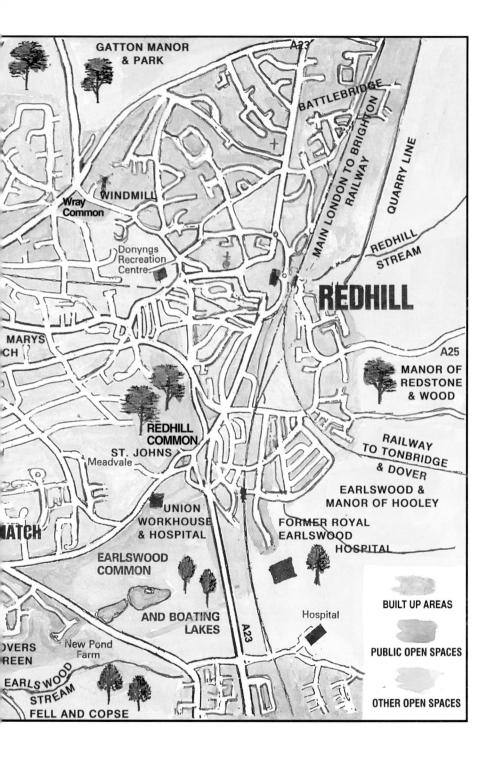

GATTON MANOR
& PARK

A23

BATTLEBRIDGE

WINDMILL

Wray
Common

Donyngs
Recreation
Centre

MARYS
CH

REDHILL

MAIN LONDON TO BRIGHTON RAILWAY

QUARRY LINE

REDHILL
STREAM

A25

MANOR OF
REDSTONE
& WOOD

REDHILL
COMMON

ST. JOHNS
Meadvale

RAILWAY
TO TONBRIDGE
& DOVER

EARLSWOOD &
MANOR OF HOOLEY

UNION
WORKHOUSE
& HOSPITAL

FORMER ROYAL
EARLSWOOD
HOSPITAL

ATCH

EARLSWOOD
COMMON

AND BOATING
LAKES

Hospital

A23

OVERS
REEN

New Pond
Farm

EARLSWOOD
STREAM
FELL AND COPSE

BUILT UP AREAS

PUBLIC OPEN SPACES

OTHER OPEN SPACES

The Angel at Woodhatch today. It was built as a bowling alley in 1612. The present name recalls the Angels on coins paid as toll fees on the old turnpike road.

New Pond, Earlswood Lakes is man made and has existed since the middle ages.

CHAPTER 5

REDHILL BEFORE THE RAILWAYS

Before the railways came to Redhill in 1841 the local landscape was very different from today. The scene was a rural backwater and a place of considerable beauty and tranquility. It consisted of four sub manors of Reigate and these were Linkfield, Frenches, Redstone and Hooley. Each of the manors would have had its own farm with cottages to house the farm labouring community.

The manor house of Linkfield stood near the present Donyngs Recreation Centre amidst a hamlet of cottages at Linkfield Street and Linkfield Lane and included the White Lion Inn, which today claims to be the oldest public house in Redhill, and a tannery. The old workhouse had originally stood at Shaw's Corner, where Blackborough mill was once a prominent feature in the landscape.

The Manor of Frenches included a large manor house beside the present site of Frenches Pond at the south end of Frenches Road. The pond was once much larger than it is today. The small cottage hamlet of Wiggie existed to the east of the pond.

Redstone manor consisted of what is today known as Redstone Hill beside the old sunken road today called Redstone Hollow. The manor house was built where the road crested the hill. Much of the hill was tree covered and known as Redstone Wood.

The manor of Hooley lay to the south east in low marshy ground near Hooley Lane. This included a few cottages in Mill Lane, then known as Water Lane because the old road descended from Redhill Common to a picturesque bridge that crossed the Redhill Stream. This is close to where the railway now passes over Hooley Lane.

To the south west lay the open common land of Redhill and Earlswood commons. Redhill Common had been the scene of two small skirmishes in the civil wars of the mid-seventeenth century when Cavaliers and

Roundheads clashed. Documents of the time confirm that the area was known as Redhill in those early days. The common is part of the ridge and today much of it is tree covered.

Earlswood Common lies further south in the Wealden district. The lower lake or New Pond was man-made in the middle ages. The upper or boating lake did not exist before the railways. It was man-made at the turn of the century. Beside the New Pond stood a brick works where bricks were dug from the heavy Wealden clay. Most of the trees on the common had been cut down by Lord Monson in the years before the civil war. Today much of the common is a golf course.

On a strip of land between the two commons is the hamlet of St. John's, once known as Little London. The older name suggests, from the origins of other areas of the same name, that the hamlet began its existence as a plague refuge in Tudor or Stuart times. Citizens of London would move out to set up residences in the country to avoid the plague.

In 1816 before the opening of the London to Brighton turnpike, (now the A23), the main west to east road along the Vale of Holmesdale ran from Reigate to Linkfield Manor. It continued up Linkfield Street and down Mill Street, along Hooley Lane and ascended Redstone Hill via Redstone Hollow. At this point it began following the present A25 along the crest of the ridge towards Nutfield and Bletchingley. Station Road Redhill and Redstone Hill below the manor house did not exist at that time.

The vale between Redhill Common and Redstone Hill is the result of local greensand being eaten away by the Redhill Stream. Today much of the stream runs underground, but before the railway it was a dominant feature of the district. Part of the stream remains visible in the forecourt of Petsmart. The stream had at least four sources from springs in the southern slopes of the North Downs. Two of these were in Merstham where the currents fed a local water mill. A third tributary joined the stream from the east to the south of Merstham. The fourth flowed from Gatton Park towards Battlebridge and may once have fed the waters of Frenches pond before joining the main stream to the north of Redhill. Southwards the stream turns to the east and runs below the ridge to Redhill aerodrome.

View from Redhill Common across the Vale of Holmesdale looking past Blackborough Mill towards the North Downs

From here it doubles back and flows into the Salfords stream which turns south west, passes under the turnpike by the Salfords Mill House Hotel and finally joins the River Mole between Sidlow and Kinnersley Manor.

To sum up, it was a tranquil, rural backwater, hardly mentioned in early history save for two small skirmishes on Redhill Common that took place in the English Civil Wars in 1648 and 1659. Dr. Wilfred Hooper, in his history of Reigate, describes early Redhill as "low lying and marshy and intersected by meandering streams, the haunt of snipe and wild duck." Let us imagine the rustic haymakers working to bring in the annual harvest and their children at play beside the babbling brooks. This idyllic scene would soon become the subject of a rude awakening.

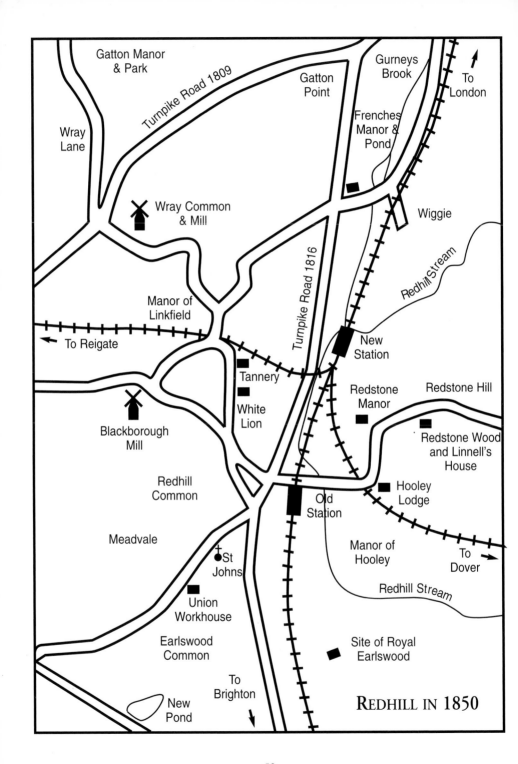

REDHILL IN 1850

CHAPTER 6

THE COMING OF THE RAILWAYS

Just off Redstone Hollow, where the old South Eastern Railway branches off towards Tonbridge, stand two rows of old council houses called Mostyn and Rennie terraces. The latter is named after Sir John Rennie who first brought the railways to Redhill. We have to question whether this is really an adequate memorial to a great man who played such an important part in our local history.

In the early years of the nineteenth century railways were equivalent to computers, planes, motorways and television in the twentieth century. They were a symbol of modern progress and the future. The railway was born in Britain and later spread abroad. At this time Great Britain was known as the "workshop of the world".

Early railways had been drawn by horses to carry freight wagons often led by a horseman carrying a flag. Experiments with early steam locomotives had taken place in the closing years of the Napoleonic Wars, led by such men as Richard Trevithick in Cornwall and George Stephenson, of "Rocket" fame. The first railway was built between Stockton & Darlington in the north east and others had followed in the north west and Kent. Soon Britain found itself in the grip of "railway mania."

The first talk of building a railway between London and Brighton was in 1823. It took a stagecoach the best part of a day to travel the 51 mile distance between Westminster Bridge and Brighton Pavillion. A railway locomotive could manage the same distance in a single hour and carry far more passengers.

An early railway construction

Ten years later the project had become more serious and imminent. The question was where the line would be and, all told, there were six proposals. Most of these, including one by George Stephenson, were designed to avoid hills and valleys to simplify the engineering and eliminate tunnels. They tended to follow a route via Epsom, Leatherhead, Dorking, Horsham and Shoreham, but Sir John Rennie persisted with the idea of the shortest and most direct route from Croydon through Redhill and Haywards Heath. This was despite the fact that it would involve considerable engineering work in terms of tunnels, embankments and a substantial viaduct between Balcombe and Haywards Heath where the River Ouse descends from the High Weald.

Following lengthy debates in Parliament, it was decided in 1837, to accept Rennie's proposal and the London and Brighton Railway Company was formed to start work on this massive and ambitious feat of engineering. The course of the old Surrey Iron Railway was purchased to form part of the track.

Laying the rails and building the stations and signal boxes was the easy part. Most of the work was involved with levelling the ground where the track needed to be laid down.

The area was invaded by an army of about 5,000 navvies to dig out tunnels and cuttings and build embankments out of soil, chalk, rock and clay taken from the cuttings. In a time when bulldozers and JCB's had not been invented, all of this had to be done by hand, pick and spade and the soil and rock carried from the cuttings to the embankments by horse or wheelbarrow and cart. In total 500 horses were used. The navvies, many of them Irish, were a rough crowd who lived in shanty towns thrown up beside the track-way and were paid very little. Most of their earnings were spent on drink and pay day was a time for fights and even riots.

It was tough, close work and deaths were not uncommon. A workman was killed building Merstham tunnel, and there are stories that a workman is buried in the embankment beside Three Arch Road near the East Surrey Hospital. By 1841 the line was ready for the first train to Haywards Heath and the line to Brighton was completed a few months later.

The first stations were built at Battlebridge, to serve Gatton Park and beside Hooley Lane where the old road from Reigate to Nutfield and Godstone was crossed by a Railway Bridge. The Hatchlands Road, Station Road and Redstone Hill we know today did not exist. The station was called Redhill and Reigate Road.

London Bridge Terminus in 1860. At that time all trains to Brighton departed from London Bridge as Victoria had not been built

*Merstham Tunnel and Redhill Station in the days when it was called
Reigate Junction*

Outside Reigate Junction with station master's houses at Betchworth and Dorking

About a year later, another company, The South Eastern, built a new line from Redhill to Ashford, as part of a London to Dover project, and built their own station at Redhill Junction. The two companies did not get on very well with each other and passengers changing trains had to walk nearly a mile between the two stations along a muddy path and cross the Redhill stream over a dangerous wooden bridge.

Eventually, the station was moved from Hooley Lane to its present site at the junction and proposals for a second branch line to Reigate, Dorking & Guildford were made. This line opened in 1849 with Reigate Station on its present Site. The station at Battlebridge was

Railway Navvie

Cartoon depicting railway mania

Brighton Beach following the coming of the railways which made access possible to everyone and not just the aristocracy

closed and re-built at Merstham. Earlswood station was built in 1868. The pillars holding up the early roof of Redhill Station had to be removed after the driver of a train leant out of his engine and was decapitated.

In 1843 Reigate's second church, now St John's, had been built on its present site because it was believed at first that the town of Redhill would be built in that area on account of the original Hooley Lane railway station. The present spire and bells were not added until 1895.

The London & Brighton Railway Company was later re-organised as the London, Brighton & South Coast (LB&SC) as lines were built to other seaside resorts such as Worthing and Eastbourne. Relations with the South Eastern Railway company were never good and towards the end of the nineteenth century the Quarry Line was built from Coulsdon to bypass Merstham and Redhill. By that time better technological equipment had been developed to cut through the tunnels and build the necessary embankments.

Early railway trains carried only gentry or first class passengers, and the second class carriages, to enable servants to travel, were added later. The third class carriages which finally emerged were, at first, no more than open cattle trucks, which meant that passengers had to contend with smoke and grit blowing into their faces from the engine. Exposed to the elements and all sorts of bad weather, travel by train in an early third class compartment often led to severe illness and in some cases death. However, in an age of reform these evils were short lived.

The railway between Redhill and Dover received some notoriety during the Crimean War as the scene of the first ever great train robbery. More recently the incident became the subject of a film starring Sean Connery.

With the coming of the railways travel to the coast was soon open to all and no longer the privilege of the wealthy. Cheap day excursions to the coast were always popular. We can imagine the trains packed with children heading for a day out on the beach with donkey rides and Punch & Judy as a special treat not to mention a stroll down the seaside piers to the sound of brass bands which were such a popular feature of the Victorian & Edwardian eras.

Extract from a 1891 Census form
Ref: RG12/0577 ED1 Folio 16(A)

60

High Street – Early Redhill

CHAPTER 7

THE DEVELOPMENT OF THE TOWNS

Since 1697, and following the Glorious Revolution of 1685, the Lords of the Manor of Reigate had been the Somers Family. They had been granted the Lordship of the Manor following the overthrow and exile of James II, who had held the Lordship of Reigate since the trial of Lord Monson in 1660. In 1806 the Manor was bequeathed to John Cocks, Baron Somers, who purchased Reigate Priory in the following year. The Somers family were Lords of Reigate until 1921.

In 1830, the neighbouring stately home of Gatton Park was purchased by Lord Monson for £100,000. The auctioneer is said to have uttered the words " Fling wide the Gates of Paradise and ye enter Gatton Park". It is possible the elaborate grounds, gardens and lakes of the park may have been designed by the famous eighteenth century landscape gardener Capability Brown.

GROWTH OF LOCAL POPULATION

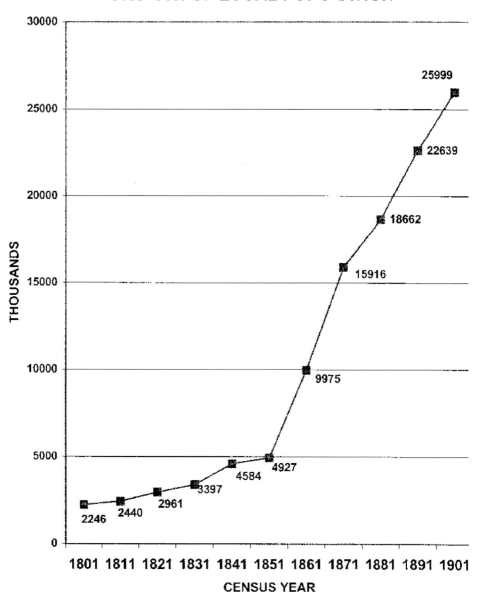

Growth of the local population from 2246 in 1801 to 25999 in 1901 according to the census returns

Back in the sixteenth & seventeenth centuries the Monsons had local interests at Kinnersley Manor near Sidlow, and Reigate Priory, during the English Civil War. It was the trial of Lord Monson for regicide that had cost the family its earlier local interests. The 7th Lord Monson died in 1841 but William John Monson, 8th Baron did much in the years that followed to fill Gatton Hall and St Andrew's Church with artefacts from around the world.

While the Somers interests were mainly in Reigate the Monsons took a deep interest in the growing town of Redhill. The early town was named after Lord Monson's mother, the Countess of Warwick, and for a time was called Warwick Town.

Warwick Road still exists on the edge of the town. Somers Road is in Reigate, near the Station and Monson Road is in the northern part of Redhill near Gatton Point.

For some years after the station was moved from Hooley Lane to its present site, then known as Reigate Junction, it was difficult to approach due to the lack of proper roads. It was Thomas Dann, later Reigate's first Mayor, who expressed the need for a new road to be built from Linkfield Corner passing the station, to the top of Redstone Hill. This is the present Station Road and no sooner had it been built than the new Warwick Town started to spring up around it including the present High Street and Warwick Road.

Note – This is the same view as on page 51 except that houses now appear between the common and Blackborough Mill

Station Road, Redhill, looking east towards the station

Draining the area of water for the building of Redhill was a considerable problem and the foundations of several buildings needed to be propped up with piles and sandbags.

The years that followed witnessed considerable development of housing in the Reigate area including many villas for the "well to do" in the Wray Park area. The villages of South Park and Meadvale were created in the old district of Woodhatch. By 1861 the population of the district had increased to 10,000 and that was only the start. The graph on the previous page shows how the population of Reigate and Redhill increased during the nineteenth century.

By this time it was possible to measure the population because of the introduction of the national census in 1801 which, from that date onwards was carried out every ten years. The census recorded every home and person and what sort of work they did. An extract of a completed local census form can be found on page 60.

Reigate had become a 'Dormitory' town where the more "well to do" working in the City of London made their homes since they could now travel to work by train. This process became known as "commuting". Building in Reigate between 1860 and 1900 included more villas in the Blackborough, Ringley Park & High Trees area. In addition terraced houses for the less "well to do" were built around Nutley Lane, the Glovers Road Estate and between Reigate Station and Doods Road.

In Redhill, the transformation around the new town was equally impressive. Both Lord Monson and Lord Somers, as well as the Ladbroke family of Frenches Manor, acquired considerable sums from the sale of land to build new housing at Earlswood. Further building took place to the south of Hatchlands Road, in the Grove Hill, Garlands and Ridgeway Road area. Other new estates were developed around Monson Road and Frenches Road. A walk around the area today can reveal the age of many of the buildings by means of date stones set in the facing wall of the house. See how many you can find.

The name of Cromwell Road recalls the skirmishes that took place on Redhill Common between Cavaliers & Roundheads in 1648 and 1659.

Reigate Borough Council was formed in 1863. Thomas Dann was the first Mayor and Dr Clair Grece the first Reigate Town Clerk. Dr Grece held the post until his death forty years later.

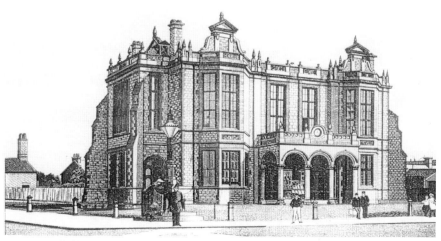

Redhill Market Hall before the addition of the east and west wings.

Royal Earlswood Hospital, formerly the Earlswood Asylum,
now converted to a private property development

The early years of the council were spent organising an effective police force for the district together with a new gas works for Redhill which were located on the site opposite the Garland Public House, and also water and sewage works. The first water works were located to the west of Park Lane in Reigate. And the sewage works were built at the southern end of Redhill Common where they remain today. The gas works were demolished in the 1970's following the new use of Natural Gas.

Amongst the early residents of Redhill were two famous artists. John Linnell, who built a house on Redstone Hill in Redstone Wood where he lived until he died in 1882, and his son-in-law, Samuel Palmer, who lived in Meadvale where he died in 1881. When Redstone Hill was developed for housing in the early twentieth century, Linnell Road and the more recent Palmer Close were named after them.

Another famous resident in the early years of Redhill was R.C.Carrington the astronomer, who lived at a house called The Dome, behind the site of St Matthew's Church, which included an observatory. Today he is recalled by no less than three places, Carrington Close off Cromwell Road, Observatory Close on the Cromwell Road Estate and the Dome tower block on the Redhill "flowers" estate off Warwick Road.

An important development in the history of Redhill was the formation of the Market Hall company and building of Redhill Market Hall in 1860. At that time Redhill had a cattle market on the site of the present Marketfield Road car park where livestock were sold and shipped onto the railway.

Lord Monson was one of the main founders of the Market Hall Company. The building was imposing and stood in the centre of the town. It included offices and general assembly rooms. It was enlarged just before the turn of the century. Its use is best recalled as a theatre where, since the early twentieth century, dramatic and operatic societies have performed plays, pantomimes & stage musicals. The hall was demolished at the start of the 1980's to make way for the Harlequin Theatre.

In 1888 the Monson family decided to sell Gatton Park and the successful purchaser was Jeremiah Colman of mustard seed fame. He would later become Sir Jeremiah Colman of J&J Colman mustard. Colman took a special interest in Redhill, especially in the numerous local working class people who lived in the area. In 1904 he built the Colman Institute as a meeting place complete with working men's recreation facilities. For a time it served as the local library. The building was demolished at the end of the 1960's to make way for Redhill's re-development and its trustees have since developed the Colman Redland Centre in Croydon Road, Reigate. Colman Way on Batts Hill commemorates this famous benefactor of the district.

St. Anne's Redhill beside Redhill Station

The development of Redhill led to the opening of several institutions in the district. These included the Royal Earlswood Hospital, which was founded in 1855. The Philanthropic School for juvenile offenders, which was opened between Redstone and Earlswood in 1849 and St Anne's Orphanage, which was built beside Redhill Station for children in 1884. It later became an old folks home and was demolished in the 1980's after the building had become unsafe.

St Matthew's Church was consecrated in 1867 to provide a place of worship at the centre of Redhill. Other Church of England Churches to open in Reigate and Redhill between this time and the early twentieth century included St Philip's (Nutley Lane), St Mark's (Alma Road), St Luke's (South Park) and Holy Trinity (Carlton Road) in 1907.

Many churches were also built for other denominations including the Catholic St Joseph's beside the Reading Arch at the southern end of Redhill High Street. The benefactor of St Joseph's was Lady Mostyn after whom Mostyn Terrace (beside Rennie Terrace) is named. Lady Mostyn lived at Hooley Lodge where Sir John Rennie lodged during the building of the railway. Early Catholic services were held in her stable yard. There were churches and meeting halls throughout the district for Quakers, Methodists, Baptists, Congregationalists and Presbyterians, the latter two more recently combining to form the United Reformed Church.

The last member of the Somers family to inhabit Reigate Priory was Lady Isabel Somers Cocks who was born in 1851 and married Lord Henry Somerset in 1872. From that time she was known as Lady Henry Somerset.

The marriage was not a success despite the birth of a son, Henry Somers Somerset in 1874. Isabel and her husband broke up and she obtained custody of her son two years later. She lived at the Priory where she held a series of glittering & glamorous parties but her real interests were related to helping the poor and people less well off than herself. Somerset Road in Meadvale is named after her and she was instrumental in opening public halls and institutions in Reigate, Meadvale and South Park.

In 1894 she founded the Industrial Farm Colony at Duxhurst near Sidlow. The colony consisted of special purpose-built homes to provide a congenial setting for inebriate women and under-privileged children. It included a church and school as well as places of work for those who lived there. Lady Henry Somerset spent much of her time working there and lived in a home called simply "The Cottage". Most of Duxhurst was demolished in the 1960's but "The Cottage" remains standing today.

Lady Henry Somerset died in 1921 and the family interests in Reigate were put up for sale. The Lordship of the Manor, park and Old Town Hall were presented to Reigate Borough Council. The Priory was purchased by Admiral Beatty and his Countess. Admiral Beatty played a distinguished part in World War I .

Queen Victoria died in January 1901 following a reign of more than 60 years. Her son Edward VII became king and the new Edwardian era had begun. The closing years of the nineteenth century had seen the invention of a machine for generating electricity and the combustion engine for the motor car. The turn of the century was the dawning of a new era.

CHAPTER 8

EPILOGUE. THE TWENTIETH CENTURY

In the twentieth century Reigate and Redhill have continued to expand. The earliest council housing was introduced between the first and second world wars and estates were built on the eastern side of South Park Village, including Alexander, Lyndhurst, Apsley and Stuart Roads and Stuart Crescent in Reigate. In Redhill similar housing was built at Colesmead to the south of Monson Road.

The events that followed were like placing the pieces of a jigsaw puzzle. The main developments of the 1930's were the building of lower middle class private housing on the Hartswood Resident's estate south of Prices Lane in Woodhatch and, following the sale of the Manor, on Redstone Hill. It was a workman digging out drains in Meadow Way on the Hartswood estate who found a stone age axe reputed to be 30,000 years old.

During World War II, Reigate was the headquarters of South Eastern Command. Tank traps can still be seen in the Castle grounds and beside the River Mole near Kinnersley Manor. The red brick pill boxes along the north bank of the River Mole at Sidlow are a reminder of these grim times. The Battle of Britain raged in the skies overhead and the caves beneath the castle grounds were used as air-raid shelters. Several bombs fell on the district, most harmlessly in the open fields but some buildings on the south side of Station Road, Redhill were hit and one bomb site remained as an ugly scar for several years after the war. There is one remaining scar on Reigate Hill which is a crater believed to be the site of an aircraft crash in wartime.

Some famous people have followed in the footsteps of Howard of Effingham and Jeremiah Colman by living in Reigate in the twentieth century. In 1821 the Priory was purchased by the family of David Earl Beatty, Admiral of the fleet and first Sea Lord, who remained a prominent resident until his death in 1936. He was buried in St Paul's Cathedral close to the tomb of Lord Nelson.

Margot Fonteyne was born in Reigate and her statue now stands in the forecourt of Watson Wyatt's offices in London Road slightly to the north of the tunnel. Melvyn Hayes lived in Glovers Road and Jean Metcalfe and Cliff Mitchelmore spent many years in the White House in Upper West Street. By far the most distinguished resident of recent years was J Arthur Rank. He was a filmmaker known as "the man with the gong". He lived at Reigate Heath and founded the Rank Organisation of which Redhill Odeon Cinema, now the Embassy Nightclub, was a part.

In the 1950's the expansion of the district began once again with massive development of Council homes in Merstham, now a part of the Borough and at Woodhatch. The Merstham estate was built to absorb some of the London overspill at a time when new towns like nearby Crawley were springing up in several parts of South East England. For a time it was administered by the London County Council, later the Greater London Council, but was eventually given to Reigate Borough Council, which was by that time Reigate & Banstead Borough Council, to manage.

Most of the new private homes were built on Batts Hill, in Redhill, or surplus land sold off by Reigate villas in the Wray Park area or, more recently, in fields that once formed the grounds of Frenches Manor and St Anne's Asylum.

The towns have changed much since the turn of the century. Most of Redhill has been re-developed and the centre of the town pedestrianised. Tunnel Road in Reigate has likewise seen pedestrianisation. Redhill today is dominated by Sainsbury's The Belfry, Donyngs Recreation Centre and the Harlequin Theatre. The area is also convenient for gaining speedy access to Gatwick Airport and the M23 and M25 motorways.

When we look back on our local history we should not forget the Reigate Pageants staged between 1913 and 1963. The first in 1913 was the Pilgrims Pageant staged on Colley Hill and consisted of a procession of costumed characters reflecting the days when "The Pilgrims toiled along the way". The second, held at the old bus garage on the corner of Bell Street and Lesbourne Road, was to celebrate the Coronation of King George VI in 1937 with Reigate Grammar School providing an episode.

The last five pageants were performed in Reigate Priory on a lavish scale under the direction of Cecile Hummel who had taught history to schoolchildren at Merstham Grange.

A Pageant of Reigate (1951), devised to celebrate the Festival of Britain, included scenes from Reigate's past - though it was a stretch of the imagination to find George Frederick Handel conducting his Water Music beside the Priory lake.

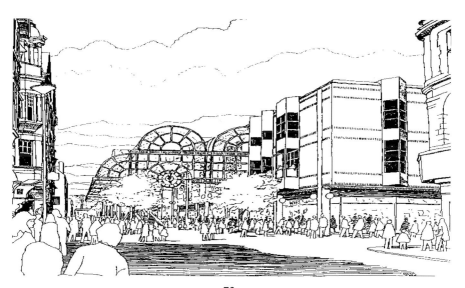

Reigate Pageant 1956. "The Legend of Chertsey, during the Wars of the Roses."
Blanche Herriot climbs the abbey steeple to prevent the curfew bell from ringing
in order to save her lover from execution.
Episode produced by Joyce Powell (authors mother)

The Heritage of the Crown (1953), celebrating the Coronation of Queen Elizabeth II, was the most lavish and spectacular of all. It was all about Kings, Queens, and chivalry. Reigate Grammar School participated with their own version of the Battle of Agincourt and despite the fact they were only using wooden swords there were plenty of genuine bruises and a few dislocated limbs.

Surrey Cavalcade (1956) included different historical scenes from all over Surrey from King John signing the Magna Carta at Runnymede to highwaymen and smugglers on Bagshot Heath. It ended in Edwardian Reigate with a horse drawn bus, a veteran car and Sherlock Holmes solving the 'Case of the Reigate Squires'.

Priory Panorama (1959) told the story of Reigate Priory down the ages from the time it was a medieval monastery, through all the families such as the Howards and Somers, to the present day. The last episodes included an air-raid and magnificent display by Priory schoolchildren in the formation of the school badge.

The Unsheathed Sword (1963) celebrated the centenary of Reigate becoming a borough and depicted, in the first episode, Thomas Dann arriving at Reigate in a hansom carriage to become its first Mayor. The theme of the pageant was the rise of democracy and included scenes of rebellion and riot with our author producing an episode that depicted Watt Tyler's Revolt. This pageant included the first train to pass through Redhill. The engine was built on a Land Rover and the carriages mounted on car chassis.

The pageants were a spectacular and colourful reminder of the past and we must never forget that it is our understanding of the past that creates a happy and prosperous future.

FURTHER READING

Reigate, it's story through the ages	W Hooper
Illustrated Handbook to Reigate	R F D Palgrave
Discovering Reigate Priory	A Ward
The Brighton Road	G Harper
The Redhill Story	Nigel Dunne
A History of Redhill (Vol. 1)	A Moore
Highways and Byways of Surrey	E Parker
Surrey Railways Remembered	L Oppitz
Down the Line to Brighton	M V Searle
A Calendar of Country Customs	R Whitlock
Brighton, History and Guide	M Sampson
Tales of Old Surrey	M Alexander
More Surrey Tales	M Alexander
The London Brighton & S. C. Railway (3 Vols)	T J Howard Turner
Smuggling in Kent and Sussex	M Waugh
Gentlemen of Merstham and Gatton	A B de M. Hunter
An Intelligence Officer in the Penninsular War	J Page
The Railway Navvies	T Coleman
Memories of Old Dorking	C Rose
Discovering Highwaymen	R Ash
The Illustrated Guide to the South Eastern Railway	G Meason
Surrey, A County History	J Janaway
The Victorian Workhouse	T May

Background Reading (Napoleonic War)

The Years of Endurance	A Bryant
The Years of Victory	A Bryant
The Age of Elegance	A Bryant
English Saga (1840 – 1940)	A Bryant

INDEX

TOPICS FOR SCHOOLTEACHERS